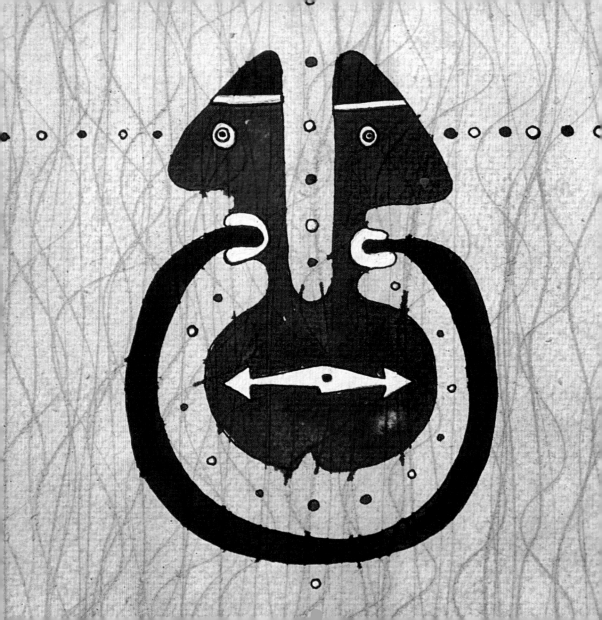

GNOSTICISM

THE PATH OF INNER KNOWLEDGE

Martin Seymour-Smith

HarperSanFrancisco

An Imprint of HarperCollins*Publishers*

A L A B Y R I N T H B O O K

GNOSTICISM: THE PATH OF INNER KNOWLEDGE

Printed in Hong Kong

For information address

HarperCollins*Publishers*, 10 East 53rd Street, New York, NY 10022.

HarperCollins ®, ®, and HarperSanFrancisco™ are trademarks of HarperCollins Publishers Inc.

HarperCollins Web Site: http: //www. harpercollins. com

1
FIRST EDITION

GNOSTICISM was produced by Labyrinth Publishing (UK) Ltd
Design by DW Design
Typesetting by DW Design in London, England

Library of Congress Cataloging-in-Publication Data

Seymour-Smith, Martin.
    Gnosticism: the path to inner knowledge/Martin Seymour-Smith.
    – – 1st ed.
    p. cm.
Includes bibliographical references.
ISBN 0–06–251305–2 (alk. paper)
1. Gnosticism. 2. Spiritual life. I. Title.
B638. S46 1996   95–33040
299'. 932 – – dc20   CIP

96 97 98 99 00 LAB 10 9 8 7 6 5 4 3 2 1
This edition is printed on acid-free paper that meets the American
National Standards Institute Z39.48 Standard.

CONTENTS

INTRODUCTION

G nosticism, the school of spiritual philosophy which flourished within and on the fringes of the Graeco-Roman world in the first two centuries after Christ, was Christianity's earliest rival. Its focus was on the attainment of a *gnosis* (a knowledge: an intuition of the truth) which brings about salvation from ignorance, rather than on belief, good deeds or contrition.

One of the chief features of this Gnosticism was the importance of secrecy. Unlike those of orthodox Christianity, its rites were practised in the the the greatest privacy. After A.D. 315, when Christianity became the established religion of the Roman Empire, the Christians sought to extirpate Gnosticism. It was relentlessly persecuted for over a thousand years, culminating in the bloody crusade against the Cathars in southern France in the thirteenth century. Now the tables are turned, for despite the savage onslaught, the symbolic and psychological truths of Gnosticism persisted in various guises down the centuries and had a profound influence on many of the great creative writers and thinkers of Western culture. Now the secret of salvation for the human condition is eagerly sought elsewhere.

Gnosticism poses burning questions, the answers to which are extremely relevant to our own day. It resonates with the notion of the psyche, with Jung's concept of the "collective unconscious," with some of the ideas embedded in the post-war philosophy of "existentialism," and with much of contemporary mysticism.

Frontispiece: The world snake, *ouroboros*, swallowing its own tail, expresses the essence of Gnostic esotericism. It is both an amulet against suffering and a representation of the cosmos, "the circle of eternal becoming," often seen with the words "One is the All."

Previous page: William Blake, the English poet and engraver, was steeped in Gnostic tradition, having learned it from Jacob Böhme and Emmanuel Swedenborg. His Urizen, depicted here in *The First Book of Urizen*, 1794, represents his notion of the "bad God"; primevally selfish, forced to contemplate himself in horror and terror, and thus to rule the world. Marcion would have recognized Blake's delineation of this hateful creator-God.

Opposite: An early-fourteenth-century fresco in the Church of St.Savior in Istanbul (Constantinople) of the *Anastasis*, or Resurrection. According to Gnostic belief, Christ's sufferings were not real: either they were endured by someone else who took his place, or he was but a phantom.

THE GOOD GOD AND
THE EVIL GOD

THE FIRST HERETICS

Previous page: This bronze hand is probably symbolic of Abraxas, whose name in Greek letters added up to 365, the number of days in the year. Abraxas represented the God of the solar year, as well as eternity. He was an eternal angel, sometimes seen as a "rescuer." In all probability his real name was a secret paraphrase of the Jewish God Yahweh, written in four (Hebrew) consonants. Abraxas is most important in the Gnostic system of Basilides.

The essence of orthodox Christian doctrine is that God, the sole creator, is absolutely righteous. Man lost the grace of this absolute righteousness at the Fall—for which he legally inherits Adam's moral liability—and can therefore be saved from it only by the Grace of God. God then sent his only begotten Son to preach the imminent approach of the Kingdom of God. And the fundamental tenet of the Christian faith is that Jesus Christ arose, quite literally, from the grave.

From the earliest days of the Church both Jewish and Hellenistic Christians defended this position with ferocious intensity. The rigorous and excitable African Church Father, Tertullian (*c.* A.D. 160–225), held that the resurrection of Christ's body—which anticipates the resurrection of everybody else's—has nothing whatever to do with the immortality of the soul. That is so undeniable, says Tertullian, that not even heretics deny it. But "this flesh, suffused with blood, built up with bones, interwoven with nerves, entwined with veins" is literally raised from death and decay: it is restored. "It must be believed," he insisted, "because it is absurd!" The unique authority of the Church is still traced to this Resurrection, this miraculous reappearance of the dead Jesus Christ.

Another representation of the Resurrection, this time attributed to Anders Palsson (1781–1849). For Gnostics, the Resurrection was simply the symbol of a cosmic event: the redemption of Sophia for the part which (in many systems) she played in the disastrous event of the Creation.

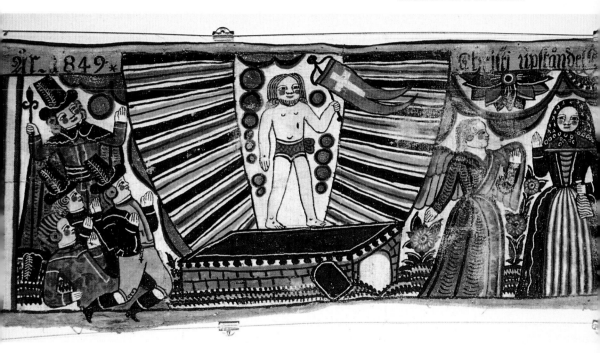

Yet so rigorous was the early Church that even Tertullian ended as a heretic. But what is heresy? How and why did such an extraordinary concept ever arise? For it was invented to the honor of the all-merciful Christian God, and it now means, simply, "any opinion against the doctrine of the Catholic church" (all churches trace their origin to the one and single universal catholic church).

In the days of antiquity the Greek word *hairesis*, meaning "choice," was applied to the tenets of the various philosophical schools. Not long after A.D. 315, when the Emperor Constantine ruled in favor of Christianity, heresy became a police matter. But the worst heretics, in the early period when no police could be called, gained the name, from their scandalized opponents, of "Gnostics." Who were they, and why, when the time came, in the Middle Ages, were they so ready to die for their beliefs? And why were their views so alarming to the orthodox that the Inquisition was set up, in 1232, to root them out? Were these views so outrageous as to deserve nothing less than death; or was there, on the other hand, some horribly unacceptable truth in them which the orthodox could not face? Those who value the Gnostic experience in modern times answer this last question in the affirmative. Either they want to learn something from Gnosticism that they cannot find in orthodox Christianity, or they seek to restore some insights to Christianity, and thus believe that the ferocious persecution of the Gnostics was a terrible error.

Perhaps the psychologist C.G. Jung was right when he declared that the ideas of the Gnostics expressed "the other side of the mind": the unconscious feelings which the orthodox, to their peril, always repress. Jung thought of these Gnostics as "the first depth psychologists."

Gnosis in Greek means knowledge, but in this context it should be translated as "insight, intuition." The Gnostic was portrayed by his enemies as a person who claimed that he had esoteric knowledge which could elevate him over other men—and undoubtedly such people, and sects, did exist, just as they exist now. Others, though, for all that they were called Gnostics, wanted to do no more than elaborate on Socrates' "know thyself": they believed that if they could look into the best side of themselves, they could discover the nature of God and of existence. Man, they believed, mirrored his creator.

Art can speak directly to the forces of the unconscious.
Opposite: Shadows on the wall flank a window of perception, in this modern interpretation by Marko Modic of Christianity's earliest rival.
Below: Hypnotic Harmony, by Marko Modic. The Creation as the mirror of the Creator.

The famous Byzantine church of St. Sophia in Constantinople, consecrated in 538. In orthodox Christianity, Sophia, far from having caused the misery of the Creation, represented "Holy Wisdom," and was identified with Jesus Christ himself.

But Gnosticism is not a single or simply definable belief-system. We ought to speak, not of Gnosticism (singular), but of the Gnosticisms (plural). However, all the Gnostic sects which flourished in the first two centuries of our era had much in common—they hated the material world, they did not believe that Jesus Christ had literally risen from the dead, and they were opposed to the God of the Old Testament, the Demiurge.

We may ask two questions. Had orthodoxy not prevailed, might not there have been (the small sect of the Mandeans, in Iraq, apart) a surviving Gnostic Church today? Or, on the other hand, are Jung's dark forces of the unconscious ever capable of the kind of synthesis we see in Christianity? Are they capable of being tolerated by official churches? Was not the Gnosticism of the first two centuries anathema to orthodox thinking because it revealed the essential materialism of the latter? We may be reminded of what Voltaire said about Machiavelli: the so-called moralists hated him not because he was wicked but because he exposed their trade secrets.

Opposite: An eleventh-century Romanesque depiction of Satan in Hell, in a tympanum over the west door of a church at Conques, France. Satan, or Yaldabaoth, was lord of the terrestrial world; the Demiurge, the evil creator-God, held sway in the Hebdomad, the "Seventh Heaven."

THE GNOSTIC FATHERS

The most lucid of all examples of early Gnosticism is to be found in the thought of the first Gnostic Father, Marcion (*c.*A.D. 100–160), a shipowner from Sinope on the Black Sea. Marcion was formally excommunicated from the Christian Church in A.D. 144.

Some have maintained that Marcion was not a true Gnostic because he was unconcerned with the fantastically convoluted speculations of such Gnostics as Basilides or Valentinus. But Marcion's system is essentially Gnostic. The orthodox Church as we know it was formed as a specific defence against it: it thus owes its very nature to it. Marcion, a gifted organizer, was remarkably successful. The Marcionite Church became the chief threat to early Christianity. After A.D. 315, with the triumph of the ortho- dox Church under Constantine, its energies were absorbed into what became the new chief enemy: Manichaeism.

Matthäus the Elder's *Apparition of God on Mount Sinai*, 1625–7. In some Gnostic systems, Moses is the creature of Yaldabaoth, or Satan. For the Valentinian Ptolemy, Moses was part-author of the Pentateuch, the first five books of the Bible.

Marcion's message, as set forth in his *Antitheses*, was unequivocal. The Christian Gospel, as set forth in Luke, is a Gospel of Love to the absolute exclusion of Law. In rejecting all the gospels except Luke—which he considered to have been written by the "Good God"—Marcion obliged the orthodox to revise their own views about the authenticity of the various gospels. He is responsible for the Bible we know.

Marcion rejects the Old Testament. There are for him two Gods, one Evil and one Good. The Evil God is the Demiurge of the Jewish Old Testament, the God of Law. He is revealed in the Old Testament as fickle, cruel, capricious, ignorant, despotic, self-contradictory and inconsistent: the Creator of Evil. Marcion acknowledges this God as the Creator-God. But, as his Church insisted, Jesus Christ, sent by the Father of Love, the Good God, came miraculously into this Creation with the specific purpose of destroying the Demiurge and of revealing the mercy and grace of his own father: supreme but remote and barely knowable. For Marcion only Saint Paul had understood the contrast between Law and Love; he therefore allowed into his canon, along with Luke, ten of the Pauline epistles.

The Greek philosopher Plato (427?–347 B.C.), in whose works many have seen one of the origins of Gnostic thinking.

Throughout the second century, Gnostic doctrines—some of these, in their early forms, undoubtedly fantastical—were in process of development. Gradually they became clearer; by A.D. 200 various Gnostic sects were, to the horror of orthodoxy, well established in every center of Christianity.

Amongst the best known of these systems were those of the Egyptians Basilides and Valentinus. Both taught full-blown mythological systems. Basilides, who taught in Alexandria, called himself a Christian, and wrote a Gnostic gospel intended to refute the orthodox ones. This, like his twenty-four-book *Exegetica*, is lost. Like most Gnostics, he gave out his teachings in a somewhat fragmentary, mainly oral, form—probably so that his followers would have to work much of it out for themselves, rather than have a dogma handed down to them ready-made. As in Marcion's system, the Supreme God sent Jesus to Earth to deliver men from the tyranny of the Demiurge; but the Jesus of Basilides, before the crucifixion, changed places with Simon of Cyrene so that he could return, "unrecognized," to his father. The view taken of Jesus was, like Marcion's, *docetic*: his humanity and sufferings were only apparent. This was another serious heresy, and most Gnostics held it.

More is known about Valentinus, also of the second century. He and his followers styled themselves "disciples of Christ." The *Pistis Sophia* (meaning Faith-Wisdom), a bizarre Gnostic text recording instructions given by Jesus to his disciples after the Resurrection,

The pagan past pervaded Christianity. This fifth-century Coptic grave slab contains the ancient shell fertility symbol as well as the Christian cross.

was once attributed to Valentinus, although it is not by him. But the more lucid parts of it could have been by him. The *Pistis Sophia*, a manuscript in Coptic (this is, approximately, ancient Egyptian written with Greek letters) translated from the Greek, tells of how Faith-Wisdom defeats the demon "Self-Will" and attains the Kingdom of Light. This document is typical of Valentinian Gnosticism. It contains passages of great beauty, and is abundant with a psychological insight lacking in the Christian writings of that period; but it is also tedious in its descriptions of the so-called Pleroma, the "upper world." The difficulty with the *Pistis Sophia*, as with the Valentinian system, is that it attempts to apply rational description to non-rational imaginative material. The Gnostics over-intellectualized, and, to make matters worse, their orthodox critics—upon whom we partly depend for information about them—not only misrepresented them, but failed to understand them. It is as if we had a richly imaginative poem, but not in its original form. Instead, we have a literal paraphrase, treating the poem as if it were just a dull set of do-it-yourself instructions.

Left: Neolithic axe, later inscribed with a carving of Gnostic significance.

The goal of the Kingdom of Light; a photo-montage by Marko Modic. Gnostic belief holds that only by plumbing the depths of the psyche can one attain enlightenment.

WINE AND FRAGRANCE

Christianity and its rival arose from the same historical situation: the first century was one of spiritual ferment and political uncertainty, in which poetry, magic and astrology vied with rational, abstract, logical thought. It was a volatile mix. A typical first-century figure was the Neopythagorean sage Apollonius of Tyana, in the Roman province of Cappadocia (modern east central Turkey). We know about him mainly from the life written by Philostratus—an unreliable but by no means negligible writer of the first part of the third century. Apollonius was born at the beginning of the first century, and survived until at least A.D. 96. He was a wandering teacher and ascetic, who visited India, performed miracles, and saw by clairvoyance the assassination of the Emperor Domitian.

Apollonius was put forward by various writers as a counterblast to Christ. What is clear from this is at least that the times gave rise to such men. Similar to Apollonius—though hailing from Samaria in Palestine—was an even more shadowy figure, who became a part of the heresiologists' demonology: Simon Magus, arch heretic. Simon Magus it is who (with later Gnostic thinkers such as Paracelsus) lies behind the Faust legend. According to Acts, chapter 8, he "used sorcery," and was regarded by both high and low as being "the great power of God." But this power is represented as having been achieved through sorcery. Simon "believes" and is baptized, but only because he wants to perform miracles. He is condemned by Peter for believing that the power of God can be purchased with money (hence the word "simony" to mean the buying of religious office).

Previous page: Third-century limestone relief of Dionysus, Greek god of wine and orgiastic excess, from a Coptic village in middle Egypt.

Opposite: The Christians described the hated Simon Magus as losing all kinds of encounters with Peter. This carving, on a capital in Autun Cathedral, illustrates the tale of how he boasted that he could fly, but fell to the ground when Peter rendered his supporting demons ineffectual.

Simon Magus reclaimed from his detractors. A modern Gnostic view, by Daniel Koubel.

This was designed to discredit Simon, whoever he may have been. He became the center of a second-century Samarian cult, regarded as a Gnostic savior. The superstitious heresiologist Irenaeus awards to Simon all sorts of magical powers, claiming that he concocted love potions, sent dreams, and evoked demons. Once (before the finds at Nag Hammadi and the advent of modern scholarship) Simon Magus, because his name is the first to appear in the context of this so-called heresy, was considered to have been the paradigmatic early Gnostic. This was an exaggeration; but he is still an important figure. Justin Martyr, the second-century apologist for Christianity, tells of how Simon was worshipped as God, and of how the woman who accompanied him, Helena, emanated from him as his "first thought." But she was revealed to be the "mother of all:" she went to the infernal regions and "created the angels and powers." The powers, having been created, then made the evil world—and imprisoned her out of envy. She had been condemned by them to wander the Earth in different bodies—including that of Helen of Troy. Then Simon Magus discovered her in a brothel, and she was redeemed.

In other, similar myths central to Gnosticism, Helena is seen as the original *Sophia*, Wisdom; the key to the origin of evil. In *The Apocryphon* (the "Secret Book") *of John*, found at Nag Hammadi in 1945, the Father of Light is above the Demiurge, the Creator God, in the divine hierarchy. In that version of the myth Sophia, daughter of the Father of Light, wished to make a likeness of herself, but did not ask permission. The result was the monstrous birth of the first demonic power or *Archon*, Yaldabaoth—the Demiurge who created the world. The Demiurge still possesses some light, from his mother; this he traps, in particles, in human creation. The quest of the Gnostic is to free these particles, and to return them to their source. The profound, frequently difficult, Gnostic myths describe the formidable obstacles in the way of the returning soul. The planets themselves were seen as archons in the way of salvation.

Contrast this with the righteous God of the Christians, for whom no such complications are possible! But many have felt, and the notion persists, that Christian theology does not fully account for the problem of evil in the world. For the Christian simple faith is enough; for the Gnostic intuition, understanding and "knowledge" are needed.

But what would Simon Magus, whoever he really was, or the author of *The Apocryphon of John*, or Valentinus, or Basilides,

A fifteenth-century manuscript of one of the most famous thirteenth-century poems, the allegorical *Roman de la Rose*. Chaucer contributed to the English translation. The roots of this long poem, written by Guillaume de Lorris and continued by Jean de Meung in a very different manner, are in *amour courtois*, "courtly love", which was, in its original form, a full-blown esoteric system based on Gnostic principles.

Shifting clouds reveal the sudden possibility of light. Photograph by Chempak.

despite their differences and their different myths, have held in common? True, for them, as not for the orthodox Christian, the world was a grim and complicated place. The powers of darkness are continually at war with the powers of light—for possession of the particles of light trapped in mankind. The material body with its appetites has actually been created to keep these particles trapped. Sexual desire has been created so that the particles will be more widely dispersed and thus harder to capture. Hence the garish emphasis, in Manicheistic rituals, on sperm.

But not all is doom and gloom. Christ came to remind humanity of its heavenly origin. Those who possess the secret understanding (open to all) can, by learning to know themselves, make a return. Moreover, the mass of people will be continuously reincarnated until they come to it. The second-century Gnostic, if we could speak to him, or her, would tell us that they alone could see existence *as it really was.*

The Gospel of Philip, found at Nag Hammadi, is a Valentinian document—probably from A.D. 250–300—which contains the positive as well as the negative side of the Gnostic picture. Although rambling and confused, it is valuable: it gives a guide to Gnostic practice inasmuch as it seems to be a set of instructions to catechumens (initiates) about to undergo their first rite; it tells us lucidly (by comparison) about what Gnostics thought about gender—that, as a scholar puts it, the "existential malady of humanity results from the differentiation of the sexes;" and it is, as a whole,

The exile of Sophia, daughter of the Father of Light. By Daniel Koubel.

A contemporary depiction of the creative power of spirit, from the College of Psychic Studies in London.

a valuable general statement of the position.

Thus *Philip* makes many Gnostic assertions. It states that "the world came about through a mistake. For he who created it wanted to create it imperishable and immortal. He fell short of his desire." This Gospel also states that Jesus came, not be be crucified, but that he "came crucifying the world." "Truth did not come into the world naked, but in types and images.... What is the resurrection? The image must rise again through the image." This last is characteristically complex and esoteric—a symbolic system—as Gnosticism always was (and is).

What it means is this. The purpose of the coming of Christ is to reunite Adam and Eve: "Christ came to repair the separation from the beginning and again unite the two." The image is of the bridal chamber; but this bridal chamber is a sacramental and spiritual one. "Fear not the flesh nor love it. If you fear it, it will gain mastery over you. If you love it, it will swallow and paralyse you." Above all, though, Philip says, the "spiritual life" is "full of wine and fragrance."

THE DUALISTIC UNIVERSE

One of the most remarkable attempts to account for the "error" by which creation occurred was made by the sixteenth-century Jewish Kabbalist Isaac Luria, who put forward the enthrallingly profound notion of the *tzimtzum*: a withdrawal of God from "himself"—in order "to make way for himself." The first step in creation is seen to be, not a step outwards, but a step *inwards*: a contraction. This is not to be confused with Sophia's desire, in the myths seeking to explain evil, to "behold herself." The notion of the *tzimtzum* lies at

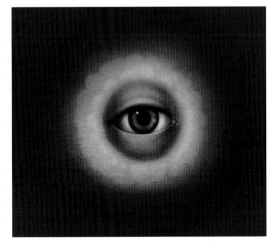

The Mystic Eye, by Malcolm Godwin.

the heart of Gnostic thinking, and, as the scholar Gershom Scholem tells us, was regarded with great caution even by many Kabbalists as "verging on the blasphemous." But through it "the cosmic process" is seen as "twofold:" "but for the ever repeated effort with which God holds himself back, nothing in this world would exist." "Every stage involves a double strain, i.e. the light which streams back into God and that which flows out of Him." Gnostic Catharism grew up in the south of France in the twelfth century, at the same time as Kabbalistic studies there were reaching their peak. That there was some secret contact between the two schools of thought is an irresistible notion.

A modern painting of Zoroaster from the Indian state of Maharashtra. Zoroastrianism continues to be practised in India by Parsees, who fled Persia after its conquest by the Arabs in the eighth century. Its rites include worship at altars on which the sacred fire burns, and exposure of the dead to vultures.

There is a kind of dualism—though it is not dualism in the technical philosophical sense—as far back as Plato, who himself saw the material world as the product of a Demiurge. In Plato, too, for all that he meant so much to orthodox Christians such as Saint Augustine, there is a hatred for the material, a desire for the spiritually perfect. And is there not a fundamental dualism of a sort between Plato's Forms and their mere copies? An inept, or possibly well Gnosticized, Coptic translation from Plato's *Republic* was among the finds at Nag Hammadi.

The classic example of dualism is Zoroastrianism (or Mazdaism), now believed to have originated in Persia in about 1700–1400 B.C. (rather than in 600 B.C.), making Zoroaster the oldest known prophet. The religion is based on the conception of the universe as a battleground of the principles of Good and Evil, although Ahura Mazda, God of Light, eventually wins the battle against his rival, Angra Mainyu. However, even in the modernized (Parsee) version of this religion, at the Last Judgment, *Frashkereti*, "the making wonderful" of all creation involves taking "literally the best" from the world of evil. It is therefore possible that this religion was originally wholly dualistic. Zoroastrianism was one of the crucial influences upon Manes, the Gnostic founder of the Manichean religion.

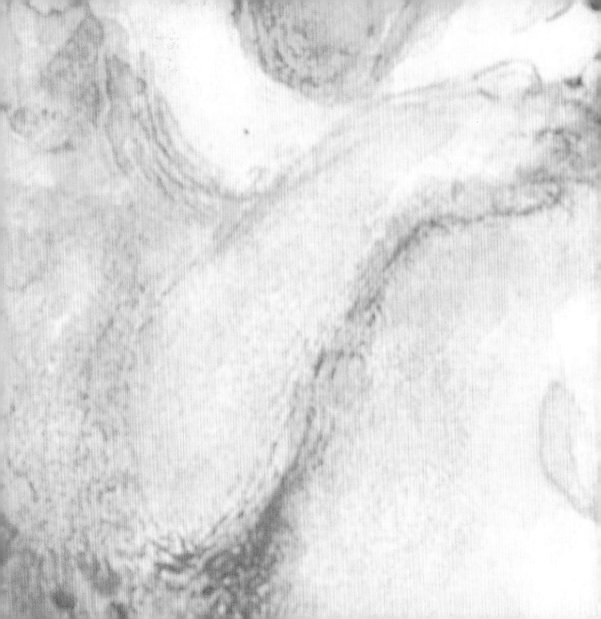

THE RAPE OF EVE

The issue of gender does not come up in *The Gospel of Philip* alone. Many Gnostics traced the problems of evil, as we have already seen, to the distinctions of gender. Although some Gnostic writings, such as *The Gospel of Thomas*, declare that "females must become males" in order to enter the Kingdom of God, others make different claims. The Gnostics showed a greater, certainly subtler, awareness of the issues of male-female equality than most orthodox Christians. In the Marcionite Church, to the unease of its opponents, there were female bishops and clergy. The late third-century Gnostic text, called by its Nag Hammadi discoverers *On the Origin of the World*, demonstrates that the Gnostics possessed insights into the problems of gender which had been denied to the vast majority of their orthodox opponents.

We may see from this how disturbing the material is to conventional minds. Part of it is devoted to the recounting of a strange myth, one which must derive from an awareness that something had gone wrong, and very early, between men and women. This part has been entitled "The Rape of Eve by the Prime Ruler and by his Angels." It is a complex, bizarre but deeply felt version of Genesis. The time is that of the creation. It begins: "Then the Authorities were informed that their molded body was alive. They were very much disturbed. They sent seven archangels to see what had happened. They came to Adam. When they saw Eve speaking with him they said to one another: 'What is this female light-

Previous page: Leda and the Cob , a watercolor by the French painter Gustave Moreau (1826–98). Moreau was patron of the Rose-Croix Salon and a founding father of the Symbolist movement in art, whose aim was to resolve the conflict between the material and the spiritual world. His paintings convey splendor concealing corruption and a palpable sense of the demonic.

Opposite: Although the artist Paul Gauguin expressed no interest in Gnosticism, his salacious *Hina Te Fatou* (Moon and Earth) may well have drawn on primitive erotic feelings about Eve's rape, hidden in his unconscious.

being? For truly she is the likeness which appeared to us in the light. Now come, let us seize her and cast our seed upon her, so that when she is polluted she will not be able to ascend to her light, but those whom she shall beget will serve us.'" It continues in this way, becoming increasingly complex. Clearly this is yet another version of the story told of Helena, "mother of all," and of how she was imprisoned "by the powers and angels" out of "envy."

Once again, undoubtedly, the Gnostic approach is over-cerebral, attempting to state in rational language an imaginatively apprehended intuition that women are not allowed by men to have their rightful place in the world. Possibly it was like that because some dangers would have been involved in an emotive presentation of such concepts, which were, as we would say today, "dynamite." And, as possibly, all the emotional side was expressed in the Gnostic rituals, delightedly represented by the heresiologists as obscene.

The rape of Eve is described with shocking force: the archangels "acted recklessly, and came to her and seized her and cast their seed upon her. They did it with a lot of tricks, not only

defiling her naturally but abominably ... and they were deceived, not knowing that they had defiled their own body." There is here, difficult though it is, a serious—and a psychological—attempt to account for male fear and hatred of women.

But, since orthodoxy regarded this kind of material as heretical, whence have we gained our knowledge of Gnosticism? Why did the Church fail to suppress it completely? Until 1960, when the Nag Hammadi finds began to be published in quantity, our knowledge depended upon hostile contemporary witnesses: upon Justin, Irenaeus, Bishop of Lyons (*c.* A.D. 140–200), Hippolytus of Rome (d. A.D. 235), Tertullian, Clement of Alexandria (*c.* A.D. 150–215), Origen (d. A.D. 253), and Epiphanius of Salamis (*c.* A.D. 315–403), the author of *Panarion* ("The Medicine Chest"), which earned him the title "Patriarch of Orthodoxy." These were the main heresiologists. They all took the opportunity to smear the Gnostics with every kind of mud that would stick, some of it so silly that it did not take in even the orthodox scholars of the nineteenth century.

Scholarly interest in the Gnostics began before then: the German Protestant theologian Gottfried Arnold pleaded in 1699 for a search for true Christianity amongst heretics; Isaac de Beausobre wrote a critical study of Manicheism in 1734; finally, Ferdinand Christian Baur (1792–1860) in 1835 made a Hegelian investigation into the phenomenon, basing his facts on what he found quoted in the heresiologists, but treating these with a new objectivity.

Opposite: This sixteenth-century representation of conflict between Sun and Moon, from the *Splendor Solis,* is alchemical in inspiration. Alchemy was only superficially a search for wealth—its essence springs from the quest for Gnostic salvation.

THE MANICHEAN LEGACY

Orthodoxy could not destroy Gnosticism even after its triumph in A.D. 315: it survived in the religion of Manicheism. The great Augustine of Hippo himself was for nine years a follower of this powerful and persistent religion—until just before his conversion. Saint Augustine's solution to the problem of evil is as famous as it is famously unsatisfactory. In answer to the question, "How can an absolutely righteous God create a world with evil in it?" Augustine rested his case on the "inscrutable wisdom of God." Evil is "the privation of some good that ought to be had:" physical evil springs from the imperfection of creatures, moral evil from free will. Manes (A.D. 216–276), however, posited a simpler and (philosophically) more satisfactory answer: opposed to the eternal principal of good, he preached, is an eternal principle of evil. Thus, good is co-eternal with evil. This, for at least some minds, is a more psychologically plausible description of the human situation.

Manes was born on April 14, 216, in Seleucia-Ctesiphon, at the heart of the Persian Empire, into a noble Iranian family. His father Pattak was a Gnostic, and he grew up in a Baptist-Gnostic sect, the Elkesaites. This Jewish-Christian group believed that an angel, ninety-six miles high, had vouchsafed the truth to their leader, the prophet Elkesai (his name means "hidden power of God"), who flourished in Syria in about A.D. 100. Manes himself began to teach in A.D. 240. In Manes we see Gnosticism in its most vivid,

Opposite: Detail from Rembrandt's *Moses Breaking the Stone Tablets*. For Gnostics such as the Valentinian teacher Ptolemy, the Ten Commandments were imperfect.

Opposite: Manes' religion, in which reincarnation—in Jewish terms *gilgul*—was emphasized, was drawn in part from Buddhism. Here is a seventeenth-century wall painting at the Hemis monastery in Ladakh of the "six stages of reincarnation."

uncompromising, and frightening, form. The Mandeans, still just surviving as a community in southern Iraq—there are, approximately, 15,000 of them—shared this background of a Baptist sect with Manes. Although Gnosticism survives in all kinds of submerged and disguised forms in our modern world, the only recognized Gnostic sect is that of the Mandeans. But these people, in great danger in modern Iraq, ruled by a barbarian, are not intellectuals, and few of them would understand the broader implications of the rituals they now follow.

Manicheism, it has been said, can be called "one of the four world religions known to the history of religion. This means, it shares a position with Buddhism, Christianity, and Islam, but, in contrast to these, lies in the past." Its founder was clearly a holy and inspired man. His orthodox critics maintained that his followers were dissolute and immoral, but it is significant that Augustine, who had been amongst them, has nothing to say on this score. However, Manes' theology is certainly shockingly scatological, being much concerned with the demonic nature of sperm.

Manes had his first vision at the age of twelve. His own phantom twin appeared to him and assured him of constant protection. At twenty-four he became convinced of his mission, as an Apostle of Light. He

A modern representation of the Wheel of Life, by Marko Modic.

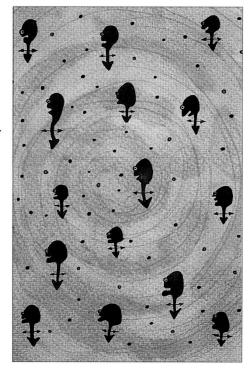

Opposite: Albion Rose or Glad Day, by William Blake, *c.* 1795. Blake in optimistic mood, depicting the emanation of Enlightened Man.

wrote: "I have come from the land of Babylon to send forth a call to the world." He formed many communities, journeyed to India and converted a king, and eventually set up his own religion at the court of the kingdom of Babylon under Shapur I (A.D. 242–273), in opposition to the established faith of Zoroastrianism (which seems, however, not to have been proscribed). He flourished for thirty years, but finally, under a new king, the Zoroastrian priestly caste, the Magi, prevailed: he was thrown into prison as a *zandik*, heretic, and, according to some accounts, was either crucified or flayed alive (or, God never having being regarded as merciful by all his representatives on Earth, both). Certainly his corpse was put on show outside the city of Belapat. But his martyrdom ensured that he alone of the Gnostics could make himself reckoned as a historical force. "The Teaching of Light" spread to Africa, Egypt, eastern Europe, China. When in about A.D. 600 it began to disintegrate, it spread in new guises: among the late-Byzantine Paulicians, the eleventh- and twelfth-century Bogomils of Thrace, and the Cathars of Germany and southern France, from the eleventh to thirteenth centuries. Manes, in forming his Church, synthesized elements from Christianity, Judaism, Buddhism and Zoroastrianism. Hans Jonas, one of the great modern scholars of Gnosticism, wrote: "[Manes' Church] was the most monumental single embodiment of the Gnostic religious principle." His teaching, in brief, is that Darkness rose up against Light as soon as, with the hatred and strife natural to it, it became

aware of it. Already Basilides and others had put forward the notion of the two opposing forces having, once, "kept to themselves." But then Light excited in Darkness Envy, Greed, and Hate, and the Eternal War began. Light was at a disadvantage, since it could do nothing injurious. "God had nothing evil with which to chastise Matter for in the house of God there is nothing evil:" in Jonas' words, "the godhead, to meet the aggressor, had to produce a special 'creation' representing his own self." In Manes' system, "Primal Man" is created, defeated, but then arises again to work out his own salvation. It was a conscientious attempt to solve the problem of evil; it may be that it was too conscientious, too dependent upon inner as distinct from outer observations, too oblivious to the go-getting nature of "politics" (not absent from official Church history), to be acceptable to the orthodox.

Manes' Church continued to survive in various parts of the world. It did not disappear from history until about the sixteenth century, by which time its successors, such as the Cathars, had already been rooted out and destroyed by those who described themselves as Christians. The Gnostic historian claims that the destroyers were merely secular materialists acting beneath the cloak of a false religion.

Gnosticism persisted, although—as the centuries succeeded each other—less in the form of open sects than in the work and writings of bold individuals such as the Humanist Pico della Mirandola (poisoned), the philosopher Giordano Bruno (burned

Opposite: A sixteenth-century German medal of the Gnostic alchemist Theophrastus Bombastus von Hohenheim, known as Paracelsus.

for heresy) and other less incautious Renaissance scholars. Bruno influenced the philosophical thought of Böhme, Leibnitz, Spinoza, Schelling and Hegel.

Gnosticism also persisted in the alchemy of the Swiss doctor and mystic Theophrastus Bombastus von Hohenheim, otherwise known as Paracelsus (1493–1541). The mystical system of Paracelsus has been called "Neoplatonic;" but it has as much in common with Gnosticism as it has with Plotinus, the third-century pagan philosopher who, although he criticized the Gnostics for disliking the material world, nevertheless contrived a system remarkably similar to theirs. Then came the Swedish visionary (and practical scientist) Emanuel Swedenborg (1688–1772), a mystic who set out to prove, by physical means, that the universe was spiritual, and who enjoyed direct contact with angels.

Protestant movements such as German Pietism—which emphasized inward religion rather than mere observance—were also decidedly Gnostic in temper. Philipp Jacob Spener, its founder, preached the priesthood of the faithful. These ideas influenced Goethe (1749–1832), the founder of modern German literature. The English artist, poet and mystic William Blake (1757–1827) was an adherent of Swedenborg—and so indeed was the nineteenth-century American Henry James, eminent father of equally eminent sons, William James the psychologist-philosopher, and Henry James the novelist.

Goethe (1749–1832), whose crucial thinking ushered in the German Romantic period in literature and music, owed much to Pietism, a Gnostically inspired revivalist movement.

THE LIGHT OF PARADISE

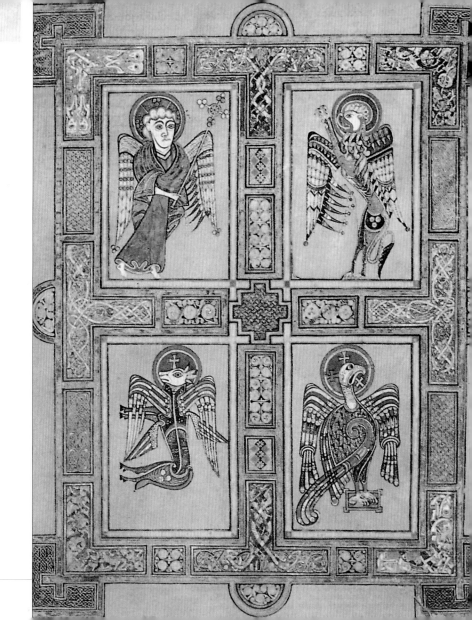

There is no such thing as a "Gnostic creed," but if, now, one were to to be drawn up, what tenets would it hold? Gnostics, fully aware of the difficulties of salvation, never advocated persecution of people for not agreeing with them. We may infer that any modern Gnostic, away from the frenetic atmosphere of the earlier centuries of our era, would preach tolerance, love and charity towards others. The *Gospel of Truth* has this to say concerning the "duties of the saved:" "Make steady the feet of those who have stumbled and stretch out your hands to those who are sick. Feed those who are hungry; unto those who are weary give repose, and awaken those who wish to be saved."

The Apostle Paul seems to have attacked Gnostics in Corinthians (mainly for their certainty of salvation and their arrogance), but, as has often been pointed out, his own thinking is not free from Gnosticism. He, too, believed in some of what would have been the main tenets of our "Gnostic creed:" that the world of Creation is fallen, and is ruled by Satan; that marriage (procreation) is dangerous, because it further disperses the light. Paul is almost *docetic* in his attitude towards Christ—emphasizing that the spiritual Christ alone is decisive. Another basic tenet of Gnosticism is its conception of life as a cyclical process, involving reincarnation or recurrence of the soul, until it is made perfect; for the modern Gnostic, therefore, time is not at all how it appears to be.

Previous page: The Angel, one of Van Gogh's last paintings. This angel is of far more Gnostic than Christian temper, being as much dark physicality as light and sweetness.

Opposite: The symbols of the four Evangelists from the ninth-century Book of Kells—Matthew (the Man), Mark (the Lion), Luke (the Calf) and John (the Eagle)—correspond to the four beasts of the Book of Revelation, and may well have Gnostic significance.

47

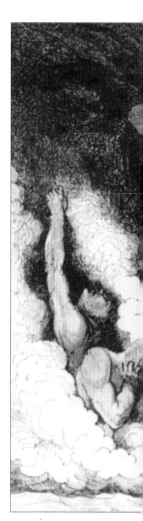

Gnosticism does not persist only in avowedly Gnostic systems. The post-war European movement known as Existentialism has much in common with Gnostic thinking. Sartre and other thinkers were, as Jonas wrote, "frightened:" their "solitary otherness ... erupt[ed] in the feeling of dread." The atheist nihilism apparent in such despairing successor-movements as "Deconstructionism," whose adherents seek to wipe out all meaning, is also Gnostic in temper; it is simply that the philosophers and the critics of the movement (which is continually changing and adapting itself and giving itself new names) lack psychological insight into their own project—they split their intellects off from their emotions in order to seem, if only to themselves, to be "objective." Like some of the Gnostic writers of old, they seek to rationalize their dread of the "other," the material, the sinister and threatening condition of nature, which that modern Gnostic William Blake said was "the Work of the Devil."

Opposite: Sinners in the eighth circle of hell being cast by demons into a lake of boiling pitch. Gustav Doré's illustration of Dante's *Inferno* graphically evokes the notion of a world ruled by Satan.

The Jewish philosopher Martin Buber attacked Jung for "locating God in the Unconscious" rather than in Buber's own influential concept of "Thou." But do we not find a flavor of Gnosticism in Buber's own thinking: in his insistence upon the necessity of spontaneous feeling from moment to moment, upon a constant inner struggle to feel towards others? Exactly the same notion, considered from an entirely different angle, is to be found in Alfred North Whitehead's Process and Reality—which led to "process theology" and eventually to the notion, easily understood by any Gnostic or Kabbalist, of God's being "dead."

Madame Blavatsky's inclusive system of Theosophy has elements in common with Gnosticism; so too, together with the ideas of Goethe, does Rudolf Steiner's system known as Anthroposophy (reincarnation is central to this), as do the teachings of Gurdjieff.

The Greek-Armenian mystic and teacher George Ivanovich Gurdjieff was a major influence on the modern human-potential movement

Opposite: Rudolf Steiner, whose thinking has exercised a powerful influence on education, evolved a system based on Theosophy and Goethe. One of the most complicated of all modern systems, it is plainly Gnostic in inspiration, and in it reincarnation plays a decisive part. For anthroposophists we choose our parents when we incarnate.

A depiction of the existential dilemma
of contemporary man, who is faced by
a universe indifferent to him unless he
grasps meaning and "salvation" from it
in Gnostic terms. By Marko Modic.

THE NAG HAMMADI FINDS

What could be more appropriate—in its mixture of chance, fraud, lying, theft and objective and scholarly curiosity—to the very nature of Gnosticism, its alien spirit, than the climax of some hundred years research into it? Above all, Gnosticism has always been characterized by its *antinomianism*, its opposition to conventional morality. Gnostics greet both the fact and the manner of the most recent Gnostic discovery as absolutely fitting. For they hold that salvation lies in self-discovery, and that self-discovery involves investigation of inevitable evil in the self—what we cannot understand, or what we deny, we can never transcend.

At the end of 1945 Muhammad Ali al-Samman, an Arab peasant, made an astonishing discovery. He found, in a cave on the side of a cliff honeycombed with such, not far from the town of Nag Hammadi in Upper Egypt, a meter-high red earthenware jar. At first he was afraid to open it in case it contained a *djinn* (spirit), who might curse him. In a sense it did contain a djinn. The whole affair was from the beginning surrounded by violence and mystery.

He and his brother had gone to dig for manure. Eventually they did smash open the jar—and in it found thirteen papyrus books, bound in leather. These they took home and put down in the straw by the oven. Their mother burned much of the papyrus: it was useful along with the straw.

1052

Third-century representation of the ancient Egyptian god Anubis, the jackal, from the Coptic museum, Cairo. The inscription is in Coptic, that is, Egyptian written with Greek letters.

Not long after this the brothers murdered an innocent man: they believed that he had killed their father. Finding this man asleep near their house, the family set to work to hack off his limbs. They ripped his heart from his body and ritually devoured it. Muhammad was worried that the police enquiring about the crime might discover what was left of the papyrus. He gave it to the local priest.

The history of the finds over the next ten or fifteen years involves liars and thieves, hitherto respectable university professors in disguise engaged in smuggling, a one-eyed bandit, crooked antique dealers, and ambitious and dishonest museum officials. The discovery seems to have brought out the worst in everyone, until Professor James Robinson and others rescued this priceless find, published it, had it translated, and made it available to the public scrutiny from which so many greedy people had wished to hide it. One may well ask why. The similar discovery of the Dead Sea Scrolls, at more or less the same time, did eventually have its scandalous elements—but never on the scale of the finds at Nag Hammadi.

The nature of the find? Fifty-two documents, translated from Greek originals into Coptic, from as early as the first century. Was this a library accumulated by zealous heresiologists anxious to refute Gnosticism? Or was it a necessarily secret collection of papyri made by tolerant, enquiring and open-minded men? The latter is by far the more likely eventuality.

An analysis of the contents revealed a few texts copies of which were already known; a little non-Gnostic material (such as a fragment of Plato's *Republic*); several invaluable Gnostic gospels; some Hellenistic wisdom literature; a *Testimony of Truth* which tells the story of the Fall from the viewpoint of the Serpent! The find confirmed what had already been suspected: that the typical Gnostic did believe that he might encounter God and the meaning and purpose of existence by a mystical exploration of himself. "Look for God," said the Gnostic Monoimus, "by taking yourself as the starting-point."

We have already seen how prevalent Gnosticism has been in the thinking of enlightened human beings. And this despite the fact that on March 16, 1244, some two hundred Cathars were burned on a huge communal pyre

Two religions coalesce in this funerary painting of a person holding the Christian cross in the form of an *ankh*, Egyptian symbol of eternal life.

(after the fortress of Montségur surrendered), and despite the Inquisition and much more persecution.

All this suggests that, whether we find that we "agree" with the Gnostics or not, we should no longer ignore what they had so passionately and so fearlessly to say—that we should, like the honorable Ferdinand Christian Baur in the early nineteenth century, pursue truth in our study of them—nor be so sure that they were what their enemies so crudely tried to say they were. Might not many of the best elements in Christianity be derived from Gnostic thinking?

It was Paul, possibly a Gnostic, but in any case the one who was not rejected by Marcion, who wrote Corinthians 1.13:2, on Charity: "And though I have the gift of prophecy, and understand all mysteries, and all knowledge; and though I have all faith, so that I could remove mountains, and have not charity, I am nothing."

BIBLIOGRAPHY

Major Works

Filoramo, G. *A History of Gnosticism*. Oxford: Blackwell, 1990.

Krause, H. *Gnosis and Gnosticism*. Leiden: E.J. Brill, 1977.

Layton, B. *The Rediscovery of Gnosticism*. Leiden: E.J. Brill, 1980-81.

Robinson, J.M. (ed.). *The Nag Hammadi Library in English*, 3rd revised ed. New York: Harper, 1988.

Rudolph, K. *Gnosis: The Nature and History of Gnosticism*. San Francisco: Harper SanFrancisco, 1984.

Further Reading

Ackroyd, P. and C.F. Evans. *The Cambridge History of the Bible*, Vol. 1: *From the Beginnings to Jerome*. Cambridge: Cambridge University Press, 1963.

Barnstone, W. (ed.). *The Other Bible: Ancient Esoteric Texts*. San Francisco: Harper SanFrancisco, 1984.

Betz, H.D. (ed.). *Greek Magical Papyri in Translation, including Demotic Spells*. Chicago: Chicago University Press, 1986.

Bianchi, U. *Selected Essays on Gnosticism*. Leiden: E.J. Brill, 1978.

Blackman, E.C. *Marcion and his Influence*. London: SPCK, 1948.

Blau, J.J. *The Christian Interpretation of the Cabala in the Renaissance*. New York: Port Washington, 1965.

Borchert, G.L. "Is Bultmann's Theology a New Gnosticism?", in *Evangelical Quarterly* 36, 1964.

Borsch, F. *The Christian and Gnostic Son of Man*. London: SCM Press, 1970.

Boyce, M. *Zoroastrians: Their Beliefs and Religious Practices*. London: Routledge, 1975.

Butler, E.C. *Western Mysticism*. New York: Gordon Press, 1967.

Bruce, F.F. *The Books and the Parchments*. New Jersey: Revell, Westwood, 1963.

Cross, F.T. and E.A. Livingstone (eds). *The Oxford Dictionary of the Christian Church*. Oxford: Oxford University Press, 1974.

Förster, W. *Gnosis*. Oxford: Oxford University Press, 1972.

Grant, R.M. *Gnosticism: A Sourcebook of Heretical Writings*. London and New York: Collins, 1961.

Hemleben, J. *Rudolph Steiner: A Documentary Biography*. East Grinstead: Goulden, 1975.

James, M.R. (ed.). *The Apocryphal New Testament.* Oxford: Oxford University Press, 1924.

Jung, C.G. *Collected Works*, 12 volumes. Princeton, New Jersey: Princeton University Press, 1953.

Layton, B. *The Gnostic Scriptures: A New Translation.* London: SCM Press, 1987.

Moore, J. *Gurdjieff.* Shaftesbury: Element Books, 1993.

Pagels, E. *The Gnostic Gospels.* New York: Random House, 1979; Vintage Books edition, 1989.

Stoudt, J.J. *Sunrise to Eternity: Jacob Boehme's Life and Thought.* Philadephia: University of Philadelphia Press, 1957.

Wilson, R. McL. *Gnosis and the New Testament.* Philadelphia: Fortress Press, 1968.

Yates, F.A. *Giordano Bruno and the Hermetic Tradition.* Boulder, Colorado: Shambala, 1978.

ACKNOWLEDGMENTS

AKG London: 12, 31, 32, 35, 36, 42, 45.
Bodleian Library, Oxford: 21.
British Museum: 39.
Champak: 22, 59.
College of Psychic Studies, London: 24.
C.M. Dixon Photo Library: 3, 7, 10, 11, 13, 14, 17, 26, 41, 56, 57.
Irish National Library: 46.
Daniel Koubel: 20, 23.
Marko Modic: iv, 8, 9, 15, 37, 52, 55.
Private collection: 29.
Juliette Soester: 49.
Theosophical Society in England: 50.
Yatri: 25.